The Edge
of
Everything

a poetry collection by

ROBYN BOURGOIN

some days I open my eyes and so goes my soul.

words pour out of me,

a waterfall of emotion transforms this energy into a part of my body, and I can't stop the tears and fears and love that appear before me.

some days I am so empty and dark,

my heart abandoned in the thought that these words may never come to me again,

it's a weight that keeps me on the banks and,

like the river needs rain,

I must wait for the moment that will take me over the edge of everything,

without these words and this place where my heart and soul open to love,

nothing I know can ever be real.

I have spent a lot of time ruminating over words to put down in these pages. Hours upon hours writing words that poured from my soul, steeped in emotion and love; inspired by my time seeking solace in the smallest spaces of the natural world. Seeing this all come together, I am comforted by the gift that my words have given me in the most difficult of times.

This collection of is truly a dedication to what my heart and life could be.

Much love,

Robyn

CONTENTS

ABOUT THE AUTHOR

ACKNOWLEDGMENTS

Special thanks to those who:

Believed in me even when I could not.
Loved me even when it was hard to do so.
Encouraged me when I struggled to go on.
Have lifted me up simply by being beautiful souls of inspiration in my life.

THE EDGE OF EVERYTHING

Part 1: A Wandering Soul
And Finding Where I Belong

My Soul is Out There

the sea, the rocks, the trees, the shore…

my soul is out there,

somewhere

moving

in the quiet whisper of the winds,

and I'd like to keep walking until I find

what I'm looking for.

My Soul is Out There

Charlestown Breachway, Charlestown, RI

Waterfalls

I can feel the way the water moves

starting smaller than a raindrop

a soft and silent course that grows with every moment,

every look   every touch   every word.

are filling the spaces of me

I never knew were empty

or maybe I did -

but I never thought there was a way through,

the rocks of heavy burdens fallen from darkness and sin

had formed their painful path.

and here is the water,

a torrent of emotions,

shining with anticipation,

aching with joy,

its flow down the river leaves nothing untouched

every crack   every hollow   every void

is filled,

with the energy of you.

it reaches the edge and

doesn't think, doesn't blink – it just falls.

tumbling down into a pool,

so deep, so filled with the memories and desire I tried to forget.

even as it takes me under,

I never want it to end.

maybe, just maybe, I'll drown in it all…

It Doesn't Think, Doesn't Blink – It Just Falls

Arethusa Falls, Jackson, NH

Dear Moon

dear moon,

standing at the promise of the sun

is what we may have known.

but after all the life I've seen,

I'll look to the moon's light,

a gentle reflection on the waters.

it silently slips into view,

reigning over the tides of my heart.

dear moon,

all your power is on the horizon,

dark seas that swell.

lights flicker and dance like stars on the water.

the deep and murky sky pauses the world in a weighted breath,

and every sigh will beg to take me away,

as I seek your softest light I stay here in the comfort of this solitude.

dear moon,

all those wishes I whispered in the wind,

did you hear them?

We Await the Light

Black Point, Narragansett, RI

Glows Like Gold

the way the sun reflects this place,

I only see your face.

I'll climb a mountain to those eyes

where they glow like gold,

warming every piece of my dark and broken heart.

the softness of the water,

each and every drop that smooths its way through,

around and under those dark and secret parts.

the hardness of the earth that gives under my step,

these places

I found in search of you

slowly changing me,

moving their way under my skin,

deep into my bones.

here I see your face and the reflections of this place,

all a ghost of what once was.

I carry on to silence in this golden glow 'til I think I have given enough

and I can be here,

at peace,

and allow the earth to take what is left of me.

Quiet Reflections on a Summer River

Flat River, George Parker Woodland Audubon Wildlife Refuge, Coventry, RI

Time Marches On

I feel a pause here in this moment.

it's drawing a breath into a silence,

so deep, profound

surrounds us in a way we've never known.

even as everything moves around us,

it seems that

time is standing still.

but time, is only passing us by

with its unstoppable force,

stealing away the little moments

we desperately hold so close.

it marches on,

not a care to who or what is in its way,

and it is suddenly yesterday and forever all at once.

we can only pray it's been enough to have these small moments,

for no matter what we do or where we go,

time marches on.

A Collision of Seasons

Frankenstein Cliff Trail, Jackson, NH

Balance of Life

we stand here,

pulled together on the edge of everything.

an almost impossible ask…

to be so tranquil, yet

caught in a delicate balance of existence

through storms at sea and winds of change

holding fast against the rising tide,

weighed down by what we've carried deep inside.

if this has shown me anything at all

I see the strength of life itself,

beautiful against the untamed sea and sky.

we'll remain here,

unflinching and brave as the sea begs us away.

willing to fall into the storm of it all,

knowing together

we will build ourselves again.

Against All Odds, We Remain

Black Point, Narragansett, RI

Awakening

deep within the darkest days, a barren winter settles in with

its icy grip around your heart,

cold seeps slowly through your veins

you try to breathe and it's the weight of an avalanche,

stealing your breath in the softness of

freshly fallen stars and the light of the frozen moon,

the day and night – so heavy and cold.

until then one day,

it's an awakening, when comes the light.

you see the glow through closed eyes

and feel the sun closer to your face.

its warmth holds you in an embrace,

the ice slips away and stirs your thaw,

the earth, so soft and forgiving,

your heart unfurls from deep within the dark and reaches for the light.

it's an awakening

and I am here.

I am alive again.

Spring Awakening

Rocky Point, Warwick, RI

Here in the Trees

here in the trees

standing in the light,

roots digging into rocky earth,

they teem with life,

hearing the worlds of many who have crossed their path,

they breathe the sigh of ages past,

have seen the years of rough and haggard ground.

here in the trees, they know me

as I struggle.

so deep-rooted,

they know my fears and heartache,

for they too have grown through ice and fire,

forever reaching despite it all.

here in these trees, I'll see my fate...

these trees may break and fall,

the most brutal upheaval of life,

flayed open,

they'll spill their roots and seeds and all the twisted pieces of dreams

are just a rotting shell of what once was

yet still, they feed the earth with no remorse

and are able to be born again.

Summer Greens and Gold

King/Benson Preserve, Wakefield, RI

Maybe Life is Like That

how long did you stay there?

deep under sea, underground,

fighting currents and tides,

tumbling and drowning

beneath the terrifying weight of the water?

how long did you suffer?

crawling through the trenches of the sea,

an expanse that never ends,

dredged through the dark sands of fear.

what valleys did you conquer?

what boulders tried to bury you?

how long did you endure the pain?

until the very sea that stole you away

found you,

carried you,

saved you,

and found a way to set you free?

and here you are now on the surface, in the sun,

polished smooth and soft as silk.

only the smallest of scars we see,

a remnant of your treacherous journey through the sea.

maybe life is like that.

When the Sea Finally Sets You Free

Mohegan Bluffs Trail, New Shoreham, RI

Come Home to Me

it was just the smallest whisper in the wind today,

moving through the trees

as I sit, so high, above it all.

here, climbing further than I ever had before.

adventure and wonder led me up at every turn

into the haze of a cloudless sky,

and those mountains

that glow with fire as far as I can see,

they are calling me softly away, here.

I can almost hear them say,

come home to me, my love,

come home to me...

A Love That Feels Like Home

Welch Mountain, Thornton, NH

All I'll Ever Be

what if all I ever were to be,

was just a passing ocean breeze.

its soft caress upon your skin,

a flicker of the suns light,

dancing on the cresting waves, and

it's warm for a moment.

I live, I breathe,

searching for my heart but somehow never found, a

permanence lost to time and fleeting moments of joy

I fear it's all I'll ever be.

a flicker of light,

a passing breeze,

one glimpse, one breath, and I am gone.

Just a Flicker of Light

Rome Point, Wakefield, RI

It's Time to Grow

it's time to grow...

despite the fear of the unknown, a future so bare, so stark and cold, where nothing stands a chance,

still,

it's time to grow.

a season of waiting, its rhythm so restless, where once the sweetest sounds would play,

still,

it's time to grow.

there's no end in sight, no hand to hold, peace is lost to the turmoil inside,

still,

it's time to grow.

sow the seeds of hope wherever it's gone, let the heart see the sun, water the soul when it is weak,

be still,

it's time to grow.

Be Still, It's Time to Grow

Cherry Blossoms, West Warwick, RI

Part 2: You
The Other Me

You

how do I know it is true love?

when asked to remember the timeline of my heart...

there is only the time before you

and the time after you,

since you,

we only measure the time between

us.

Signs of Love

Shelter on the Ben Utter Trail, West Greenwich, RI

And Here We Are

I spent my life searching, hoping, wishing, never really knowing—

thinking it would never be.

and just when I thought I could never love again,

you walked into my heart and opened my eyes.

you made me feel and made it real.

the world around us could burn, burn so black and so bright, collapse and fall

away.

and here we are,

our souls laid bare, a force beyond compare.

all the stars exploding in our eyes,

and we can't comprehend the love that consumes us.

you've spent your life searching, hoping, praying, never really knowing—

thinking it would never be.

just when you thought you'd never love again,

I walked into your heart and opened your eyes.

gave you a love that changed your world, your sweetest girl, forever and always

yours.

our souls are seen, our hearts entwined with love.

we can't go back to where we were before,

but we won't ever know what comes for us in the end.

and here we are.

Finding My Way to You

Footbridge over Flat River, George Parker Woodland Audubon Wildlife Refuge, Coventry, RI

Surrender

I had to give up trying not to love you.

surrendered myself to love,

and now I simply pray:

that far across this endless sea,

somehow our lives will find a way,

as we love with this passion, so unceasing.

and even now without really knowing the end,

I still pray

that through it all,

we will love forever with this fire for the ages,

and always embrace,

the perfect joys of today.

Say You'll Wait for Me

Scarborough Beach North, Narragansett, RI

All I Ever Wanted

I think should like to watch the sun rise,

to walk with you in silence,

our weighted breath,

in the midnight air, then

twilight stirs, it's blue and pink and gold

the scattered stars to light the way,

I'll hold your hand,

we'll sit in peace and count the moments in our quiet breaths

'til the sun slips into view,

carefully moving with purpose and grace

glowing with all its warmth upon your face

I see your light, dancing in the sky and all across the sea

it's like a dream, higher and higher we rise

my joy, my love, my hope, my everything,

is all I ever wanted and it is here.

it is all right here.

It Is All Right Here

Rome Point, Wakefield, RI

Never Enough

if anyone has ever said

just

one kiss

was ever enough for them,

then I know that they simply have never felt

the

breathtaking

      soul-moving

          intoxicating

              electrifying

                  desperately-seeking

kiss.

from deep inside us

      burning like a wildfire

          shattering the earth

              crashing to shore in our windswept storm

                  our very breath makes time stand still,

like it is the first time and maybe even the last time

this kiss will ever be.

just

one kiss…

is never enough.

One Kiss and I Am Overflowing

Basin Cascades, Lincoln, NH

No Man's Land

you know where I went today?

I went back to no man's land,

the place I went to,

never quite knowing what I would find.

I didn't know I would find you there

in no man's land.

but now that I've seen it again,

I know;

that's not where I'll leave my heart.

this no man's land is for us no longer.

you can take my hand

and we can leave this place,

even without knowing the end.

Whispers of Love

Sand Dunes, Coventry, RI

A River

your heart is a river,

love is flowing over me and

it's the sweetest love I've ever known.

After the First Dawn Rises, So Does My Love For You

The Pemigewasset River, Lincoln, NH

Our Song

are those lyrics to a song?

I don't know…

maybe it's just a song that needs to be written.

we can take all these words,

a collection of treasured memories

overflowing with everything joyous and good

and stitch them back together

in a careful arrangement of tones.

our hearts, a love-filled melody.

our dreams, play out loud on threads of gold.

forever entwined in everything we know and desire,

so the world can hear the way our souls soar like we've known it all along…

we can write the story of us in a song.

Our Dreams Play Out Loud on Threads of Gold

Browning Mill Pond Trail, West Greenwich, RI

Holding the Light

one day I found the smallest glimmer of love

and what life must be like in your light.

I cling to that hope…

even as it is so futile

to hold this gleam of light so close,

against it all,

but here I am,

and I won't ever let you go.

Delicate in My Arms

Sunrise Drops of Dew, Narragansett, RI

Find Me in Your Sunbeam

find me in

the softness of the water…

its cool and gentle currents,

they cover me,

pour over me the memories steeped in every swell.

find me in your sunbeam,

the light that warms my heartbeat,

glitters its way through the ripples

pooling their way around me.

I'm listening to the rush ahead,

the currents unknown that beg to steal me away,

right over their rhythmic cascade.

here I am safe to remain in this place

that shines with possibility.

will the water wash it all away?

the darkness in me that stayed too long,

even as I might imagine

those layers falling away will reveal a deeper twilight.

hope remains here and under your light,

alive in my heartbeat,

moving in the pools of love from your eyes.

one day that quiet cascade, so far from here,

may bring me home.

Find Me in Your Sunbeam

Wood River, West Greenwich, RI

I Carved Your Name Upon My Heart

in the quiet moments of the darkest night,

under the softness of the stars,

I hide myself away and find the place

where I carved your name upon my heart.

I trace every letter softly as your hand in mine,

every jagged line, every breath, every touch,

I'll remember every moment

I bled for you in the name of love.

these scars are mine and mine alone.

I felt everything in that euphoria,

hurting only when you were gone,

and the sweetest everlasting love I know will remain inside me,

just under the surface of your name

that's carved upon my heart.

I Carved Your Name Upon My Heart

JB Hudson Trail, Arcadia, West Greenwich, RI

It Could Be Like This

this river runs through my heart

flowing over the rocks of my past,

smoothing the edges, little by little,

its waters nourishing my soul

cascading through every part of me I ever thought was lost.

I see you,

far away, an ocean of love in your eyes,

the salt from your sea,

its waters rise and overflow,

torrents reaching streams from the mountains above

until the river of us has found its way here.

and here we are now in this moment,

and all I see is the sun in your eyes as it sinks beyond the highest peak.

the way its gold reflection glows across your skin,

your hand that fits perfectly in mine,

the joy inside radiating warmth against the breeze.

you look back at me

with such acceptance in your eyes,

and so much peace fills my heart

that even the mountains seem to say…

it could be like this.

Reflections of Peace in My Soul

The Pemigewasset River, Lincoln Woods, Lincoln, NH

Everything and Everything

when you're standing at the edge of everything and everything

is so high so far

so thinly veiled in grey and blue,

its unending depth just takes all your breath away.

looking out there, so far away

you could cry at its expanse,

it's both a promise and a burden to be safe on the edge and

yet afraid to fly.

somehow love in your heart has soared,

it's found you out there, in the wilderness.

it's everything, you thought you died from

it awakens in your solitary life.

this love, it has taken your soul into flight –

it cannot be contained,

and from your own silent depths

the urge to jump into the unknown is so real.

it would only take a moment of surrender

to take that hand forever,

step away from the edge

of everything and everything,

then fall away and fly.

What Waits for Me on the Horizon?

Black Point, Narragansett, RI

You Are the Gardener

I bloomed under your gentle hands,

tended with sweet words of love.

every kiss you gave quenched my thirst,

and I shone brightly under a light filled with love.

tend to me, love,

tend to my heart

the love you give, that love like no other, was everything I needed to grow.

but I am the flower,

and you are the gardener.

my roots have spread deep and you can't just simply pluck me away.

tend to me, love,

tend to my heart.

to go too long without your care

my only fate is to wither away,

my spirit closed tight,

a brittle and faded reminder of my heart before you.

if I could hold you somehow forever,

hold tight to the tenderness and love,

but I am the flower,

and you are the gardener.

Your Sunflower Blooms

Hodgkiss Farm, Jamestown, RI

Sunflower and Sunshine

I caught a glimpse of her in the garden today,

hair glowing in the gentle winds,

a reflection of all the flowers that turned to face the sun and her.

I see her eyes, shining like the skies on a bright summer day.

they light me up with love I can't contain.

I see her smile, leaning in to brush her hair along the soft petals of the sun,

a lifetime of simple treasures that await.

how can anything else compare?

when she turns to look at me,

in that moment,

I see her for all she is and ever will be,

everything and always

my sunflower and

my sunshine.

May You Always See Yourself How I See You

Hodgkiss Farm, Jamestown, RI

Send Me an Angel

I asked God to send me an angel

and maybe, just maybe,

knowing how long it had been,

he did.

but here,

just in one look I knew,

I didn't need an angel   —

he'd sent me you instead.

somewhere out of the dark that once was...

my heart is unfurling in the warmth of your glow,

seeing our world inside your eyes,

breathing in every word kissed by the morning dew.

I gave myself to love and you,

scattered all the little pieces of my soul and you gathered them up and spun them

into gold.

How You Saved Me

Browning Mill Pond Trail, West Greenwich, RI

Part 3: Broken
All The Little Pieces of Me

Heart of Stone

be careful what you promise her

for her heart is made of glass,

a transparent vessel, delicate and open to the world.

her heart of glass makes it easy to glow in the light of love,

its prisms glimmer and flicker their way through the shadows.

be careful what you do with her

for if she lets you inside her, you will know,

you'll see what she doesn't say aloud.

every little vein   a crack

every scratch   a memory of the words and pain of unfulfilled promises

every impact   no matter how small

ripples tiny fractures wherever that glass is unbroken.

be careful what you say to her

for enough blows and that heart could break,

shattering into a million pieces tiny as grains of sand.

one breath and she's scattered in the wind,

so far gone from herself, a bolt of lightning couldn't bring her back.

perhaps one day

she'll have the time and the will to gather herself again.

but you'll have to be careful

for if she returns to you   —

her heart will be made of stone.

My Heart in You

Found on Mohegan Bluffs Beach, New Shoreham, RI

The Burden of Love

there's a freedom in love,

to open your heart,

to feel the joy,

and see the good,

and imagine a life,

and find all the beautiful ways to say...

love.

but when the world changes,

and pain reveals itself,

digs deep to the core,

darkness creeps into the space

where light once was.

all the fear, the hurt, the emptiness,

seeps through your veins

until you can't even stand to open your eyes,

and yet you remain there,

yoked to the belief that this...

this is the right thing to do,

and I suppose it is,

to love   despite the change

to care   despite the sadness

to see there is only a glimmer of hope so dimly in the present

knowing it would glow like fire in another universe.

and that, my love,

is the burden of love.

Too Heavy to Carry Home

Mohegan Bluffs Beach, New Shoreham, RI

Solid At Your Feet

I am the rocks at your feet,

I never change, won't ever change.

you are the water,

a never ending,

ebb and flow of energy,

you let the heart decide,

when you may be the smallest of streams, a raging river, or the deepest ocean tide.

and yet as we meet,

I, the rocks at your feet

and your waters flow,

our worlds collide,

and no matter how strong, how weak, however changed

your water may be,

I am still here,

solid at your feet.

the turbulence carving through me,

wearing away a path to nowhere.

though there are days your waters run dry,

I will remain.

I am the rocks at your feet,

I will never change, won't ever change.

You Are the Water

Sabbaday Brook, Conway, NH

Tear You Up

if I remember all those moments

and write it down today,

I'd fill a book with those words,

impossible to run out of ways to say

I love you.

and I'd name that book

you,

keep it hidden away in a secret place

where no one would ever see

or tear you away from me.

when that day soon comes and our time is gone,

love

is no longer something we can say out loud,

and the only thing I think to do is to tear you up and let you go,

let all the pieces of us be taken out to sea,

forever etched in those endless pages

our treasured memories.

Impossible to Run Out of Ways to Say

Beavertail Lighthouse State Park, Jamestown, RI

Let Love Go

I wish I could learn to let love go.

the idea that even as it could be so easy to love,

to stay with you in the sweetest embrace,

life just doesn't work that way.

but I see you - I feel you

and love pours over me

      like a waterfall,

fills me,

pulls me over the edge of everything

love,

your hand holds tight,

your heart in mine.

time stands still,

every moment pours over me

      like a waterfall,

here on the edge

I close my eyes and

still

see

you…

I wish I could learn to let love go.

I Close My Eyes and Still See You

Gem Pool, Ammonoosoc Ravine Trail, Jackson, NH

The Space Between Words

it may almost seem we have run out of words to say

voices trailing away…

a stilted way about us,

lost to know what is right and what is gone.

love,

try to remember what is in the heart

and the moments of it all,

when there's a space between our words

we may always know

it is not truly gone.

what it is

that's left unsaid…

the space between our words.

A Stilted Way About Us

Camp Varnum, Narragansett, RI

Imagine

I imagine myself telling you all these stories,

wishing you were here.

I see the words

and feel it all with every piece of my heart,

these moments of beauty that fill me with love and life and

yet,

you are not there...

I'll imagine myself just doing this always,

the only way I'd ever get through,

to hold you close in my heart and tell you these stories

of moments that fill me with life and love and

yet,

you are not there.

Wishing You Were Here

Black Point, Narragansett, RI

Slay My Heart

I need to slay the beast that lies within

and silence its painful roar.

I have found for too long that this beast cannot be tamed,

it cannot be outrun

its voice screams at my spirit,

overwhelms everything I feel and

betrays my strength.

every time I think I've won,

that roar returns,

and I lose myself all over again,

but I know I cannot live in this fear forever,

if I could cut away every layer

of life and love from its heart,

let it all bleed away,

I'd find in the crimson that pooled under me, a way out.

I could dive deep into the hurt, the loneliness

and tell the lifetime of disappointment I am better bathed in its blood.

the weaker the beast, the stronger I will be

if the only way I can find my peace is to lay it all to rest,

drained and in the ground

then slay the beast,

and slay my heart,

so I can finally be free.

A Way Out

Black Point, Narragansett, RI

Letting Go Was the Hardest Part

love is weaving its way through every piece of me,

and every day I want more to give, more to live,

and I fear through it all,

this love for you,

I had simply no right to ever give…

I'll never know where we could go

beyond the now and into the light

with you in my heart.

every day is a gift, a treasure,

the sweetest pain I can't escape.

even as I know—

there's a day of reckoning to come.

will we say our story was written in the stars?

or will we say

letting go was the hardest part?

Every Day is a Gift

Conimicut Point Beach, Warwick, RI

I Will Not Possess Your Heart

I am the sea,

raging waves and quiet tides pulling you into my arms and under, I hold you close,

your strength is my weakness - it lives in me

I cannot let you go.

deeper and deeper we fall into the storm

I cling to all I know and love,

yet I can feel it slipping through my grasp

it's washing away along my shores...

I will not possess your heart.

I watch and wait for you, for me

drawn deep into your eyes, unmoving at your shores, the power of your waves

reaching for anything that feels like home, what rock may ever save me,

but it's with you

your salt under my skin, the storms of uncertainty and curses of our sea

my heart is in you

your strength is my weakness - it lives in me

I cannot let you go.

through all the storms you've drawn me in and loved me

still

I cannot find a way beyond your sea

and I cling to all I know and love

but its slipping through my grasp...

I will not possess your heart.

I Am The Sea

Black Point, Narragansett, RI

Never Let Me Go

when I placed my heart inside your hands,

I let you see where no light had ever been.

my spirit flew so high with love

and I never wanted to land.

was there a day you promised me?

that I would always be, your sweetest girl,

you'd never let me go.

it wouldn't matter now,

here I am, an empty shell of me,

broken pieces,

falling desperately.

clawing at anything to save me, then

willing myself to sink into the darkest parts of the sea...

was there a day you promised me?

that I would always be, your sweetest girl,

you'd always know,

you'd never let me go.

Falling In The Deepest Parts of the Sea

Scarborough Beach, Narragansett, RI

An Ash-Filled Sea

I can let you tear down these walls

burn them to ash and lay them out to sea.

I can give you my heart,

a gift of love in a song,

and we can change our destiny.

one moment in time was all we needed

even as we may have known,

that my heart, my soul, my love was meant to be yours,

it was always meant to be yours.

and yet, a love-filled destiny or not,

my life may never be yours to have.

what happens in the end?

when all is lost and

I've given you so much of my everything,

as I face the world with nothing left inside,

how do I rebuild these walls with all the pieces of me floating away in the sea?

Searching Between the Tides

Beavertail State Park, Jamestown, RI

Loving Me, Loving You

this is the price I've paid

for loving me, loving you.

this fleeting way,

all our darkness exploding into light.

this infinite joy, its edges dipped in secret sorrow.

it breaks me down again and again, and instead of walking away…

I am here,   entrenched in the deepest love.

I stay,   drowning in the waves.

I beg,   the blackest of night to cover me,

in rest…   and underneath it all the stars will light my way free

so I can finally

breathe

again.

this is the price I've paid,

little pieces of me left behind,

a trail of wishes and regrets,

left to me, left to you.

I'll wait forever for just a taste of you,

to last a lifetime under my skin,

brighter than the stars and deeper than the sea,

more than anything I've ever seen.

somehow, I know it, the love is still there, somewhere,

but now I reach out to you and I only feel air.

and this is the price I've paid

for loving me, loving you.

Under the Light of the Moon

Moonstone Beach, Charlestown, RI

Let Me Lay in My Grief

let me lay in my grief for a moment

so I can close my eyes and remember,

a quiet whisper of love will remain in my heart forever.

I can cherish the memories of your voice and the way it moved me,

your kiss   and the way it filled me,

your touch   and the way it electrified me,

the softness,

the kindness,

the absolute purest of loves.

let me lay in my grief for a moment

so I can close my eyes for a moment longer than I had you and remember.

a life that may never be will play behind my eyes,

mourning the tragedy of a life not lived before death,

the alternate life that never was,

where I cherish the moments of everything and everything that made my

world a different place because of you.

just let me lay in my grief for a moment and love you.

Who Sails Beneath These Clouds?

East Ferry Beach, Jamestown, RI

Sleep and Wake

I am afraid,

I am somehow starting to forget.

how it feels to be in your arms,

under the warm caress of your love,

the trail of fire you've left beneath my skin,

the way you found your way into every part of me,

as we tumbled our way into darkness.

it is a softness, a powerful force, the deepest longing, and

it's left me breathless and bare.

has it been so long, that I fear it is only a dream I found somewhere in the space between awake and sleep?

here, I am most alive,

I am warm in your arms, your love, your peace, your heart is here it's all so real,

I can breathe, I can feel,

and yet I sleep and wake and I am still - breathless and bare,

suddenly so afraid

I am starting to forget you.

I Don't Want to Forget These Days

Pemigewasset Overlook, Albany, NH

You Are With Me

I wish you could see it,

the way the clouds move on the far away horizon.

the shades of blue and pink,

they cover the sky in softness on the jagged edges.

I wish you could hear the silence,

the air so still it's like the mountains have paused their breath for just this moment.

not even the smallest of dew drops dares to breathe through the blades of grass.

I wish you could see how the sky is changing from midnight, to pink, to gold,

as the horizon deepens in sapphire, ablaze with light.

I try to count the trees as they glow, but they go on forever.

as the sun rises, I swear it's the warmth of you near me on this edge and you're not

so far away.

I wish you could sit here with me and know...

here in this moment,

you are with me.

The First Sunrise

Hancock Overlook, Kancamagus Pass, Lincoln, NH

THE EDGE OF EVERYTHING

Part 4: The Infinite Horizon
And Every Possibility

White Shadows

I keep waiting for this feeling to pass,

through the darkness we fell together

in a pool of white shadows,

drowning in each other — we only see us

pulled together in a way we never knew before

your voice, your hand, your love,

the only real that is here when we can't see through all that hides us in the shadows

I keep waiting for this feeling to pass,

to feel less in the rage of heartache and infinite joy,

the constant companion of letting love become the escape in these white shadows.

it's beyond anything we can control

together or apart, time spent or not.

we are the same, the energy that flows and grows

through us as we love here in the shadows.

I keep waiting for this feeling to pass,

to wake up one day and say it's time to let go,

free fall my way back to darkness that existed before you and us in the shadows.

for as long as I can, I'll hold you close in this moment,

breathe in this intoxicating air and pray

enough of you remains inside me to go on, as I make my way through,

your voice, your hands, your love,

here in the shadows.

I Keep Waiting for This Feeling to Pass

Black Point, Narragansett, RI

To the Sea

in all that's left to the sea,

words and love and life itself.

they are here, only in a memory.

they rise and fall,

so lost within the deepest tides.

let darkness take it all,

where on the horizon it seemed so free,

in the end, it was never meant to be.

take all the light from the setting sun,

and leave love to the sea.

Take All the Light From the Setting Sun

Moonstone Beach, Charlestown, RI

It's Like Holding on to Water

for the things I cling to when I'm sad,

it's like holding on to water

all the little drops of you that cool me

are the same that fill me, cover me, drown me.

the warm currents that take me gently out to you and the sea

are the same that crash me on the shore relentlessly.

if I stay too long here, those depths will take me under,

breathing in the darkest place,

currents leading me too far from you,

all my light will be lost, spilling through my fingers like water.

breathe me in,

wash over me with that weightless love

a reason to fight on, and I'll have

something real to hold

I can pull myself to shore

and put my feet safely on the ground.

for the things I cling to when I'm sad

it's like holding on to water.

This Morning Light

Black Point, Narragansett, RI

This Love Sinks Ships

this love;

we feel so deep inside us,

a love so profound,

raging like the storms at sea,

a dark and twisted place.

these storms,

they carry all our rage in heartache,

an unpredictable and dangerous existence.

we feel a madness so intense,

so deep inside…

this love.

and the waves,

they churn and grow with every swell of fear and unknowing and

sink the ships of men, leave their bones

to the rocks below in an endless watery grave…

raging on in heartache,

these storms at sea.

Our Rage in Heartache

Black Point, Narragansett, RI

The Sea, She Calls for You

with every breath, the sea,

she draws you in, tempting you with her siren song.

her waves like dampened tendrils, reach for you,

so soft and warm, slip silently into your grasp.

an intoxicating breath, as never before…

she pulls you into a cloak of warmth.

beneath the foam you see the light on the surface

so clearly, the glittering relief of air.

she holds you close, so soft and warm,

her waves spiral and flow; they reach for you,

slip silently around your heart,

sinking you further into the darkness.

the sea, she calls for you, she begs for you.

her waves, they've drawn you in too far.

her song, a haunting melody of pain.

her love, lost at sea forever.

she cannot fathom what she has done,

and with every ebb and flow of tides

under the sun, under the moon she cries,

a whisper in the waves

return to me…

return to me.

Return to Me

Black Point, Narragansett, RI

Her Song

a siren from the sea,

her shadows in the mist,

her song swells from the darkest depths

finding its way to your heart.

after all these years

she is everything and everything you seek to find

wandering waves of turmoil and fear.

she is there with you,

finding your soul in her beacon of light.

she will breathe life into you once more

fill your lungs with the salt from her tears as she cries.

for even as you say: you are mine.

the waves will rise and pull her from your arms and

she can be yours no more.

her heart and soul remain with you

but her song belongs to the sea.

Her Song Belongs to the Sea

Black Point, Narragansett, RI

Breathless in Between

how do I take a moment to breathe?

knowing you are there

and I am here…

where every breath is for you and

the space between us.

and here?

I am breathless,

crossing our endless horizon

just to breathe you in once more,

taste the sea in my lungs

and hold it deep inside,

knowing

each time could be our last.

and the space between us never ends.

taking a moment to breathe?

no.

knowing you are there

and I am here

I am breathless

in between.

This is Going Home

Conimicut Point Beach, Warwick, RI

We Are Bound

we are bound—

you and I,

bound to each other

the way the sky is bound to the sea.

in an endless horizon,

currents that draw us in

stronger and deeper still,

it's the only place we can be.

to find us,

one need only search the waves,

a steady rhythm of the heart.

like salt in the sea,

adrift in each other,

we become one and the same,

the only place we are free.

we are bound—

you and I,

the way the sky is bound to the sea.

Like Salt in the Sea

Black Point, Narragansett, RI

Where the Mountain Meets the Sea

I imagine a world where the mountain meets the sea.

where love exists openly,

despite the tides of life that ebb and flow in chaos

in every place along these shores,

the strength of where they meet grows

in the most impossible way;

even where it seems there is no answer to it all.

blue, so blue is the water against the vibrant greens of the mountain,

waves shining in every reflection with love, and

the trees, they breathe through the wind,

reaching all the way to the deepest parts of the sea…

in this world, where the mountain meets the sea,

there is no rest, no end, no final vow,

only the promise of endless love...

always everything and everything,

no matter what the tides may be.

Where the Mountain Meets the Sea

Beavertail State Park, Jamestown, RI

Waves

waves, follow the rhythm of my heart

safe on the shore

where we lay,

I don't hear it at all.

I can feel you with every breath...

salt filling my lungs,

my bones,

they know I am home here

with the waves

flowing through our tides,

stronger, as we go deeper over the edge of everything

every beat of my heart is for you,

how I prayed for you,

I should have waited for you.

I hold you close to me

against the waves, I fear

they'll only take me under,

yet they follow the rhythm of my heart

under the light in our sea,

we pray,

here we are home,

and here we will lay.

We Are Home Here in the Waves

Charlestown Beach, Charlestown, RI

How to Breathe

sometimes I think I may have forgotten how to love,

how to feel,

how to breathe.

I get so trapped in the darkness of my heart

unable to set myself free.

I let myself out to sea and

then I see you,

and the way your light shines in my eyes,

the steadiness in your tides,

your essence seeping under my skin,

and I know somehow it will all be real again

if you only bring me to shore,

to love,

to feel,

to simply breathe you in.

I Let Myself Out To Sea

Rome Point, Wakefield, RI

I Wish You Could See It

I wish you could see it.

the way the mist eases its way off the waves,

blurring the air in a hazy glow.

the way the sun sparkles on the surface,

ripples reflect the pink and blue and gold.

I wish you could hear the waves as they rise from the horizon,

they draw their power from deep within,

crashing in a rhythmic beat on the shore.

I wish you could feel the way the salt air seeps into your skin,

wind grazing your face as it pulls you in and you taste it with every breath.

as the sun rises, the light is warm and bright,

and I swear I can feel your arms around me.

I wish you could sit here with me and know.

here by the sea

you are with me.

Here in this Moment

Black Point, Narragansett, RI

ABOUT THE AUTHOR

Robyn Bourgoin is an artist, poet, avid hiker, and hobbyist photographer.
A lifelong New Englander, she now resides in Rhode Island with her family and
beloved family dog.
The Edge of Everything is Bourgoin's first poetry publication.   .
When not attending to her children and her home, Robyn can be found most often in
her basement studio with her headphones on, or getting up at ungodly hours to watch
the sun rise and commune with the Rhode Island coast.
She is a free spirit, adventurous, and always striving to find her magic.
To learn more, you can find her at:
www.aninspiredoutlet.com

Made in the USA
Middletown, DE
04 October 2021